NIGHT
MUSIC

NIGHT MUSIC

Selected Poems

John Clellon Holmes

The University of Arkansas Press
Fayetteville   London   1989

DESIGNER: Chiquita Babb
TYPEFACE: Linotron 202 Granjon
TYPESETTER: G & S Typesetters, Inc.
PRINTER: Thomson-Shore, Inc.
BINDER: John H. Dekker & Sons, Inc.
The paper used in this publication meets the minimum
requirements of the American National Standard for
Permanence of Paper for Printed Library Materials.
Z39.48–1984. ∞

LIBRARY OF CONGRESS CATALOGUING-IN-PUBLICATION DATA

Holmes, John Clellon, 1926–1988
Night music.

I. Title.
PS3558.03594N5   1989
811'.54   88–20648
ISBN 1-55728-067-3 (alk. paper)
ISBN 1-55728-068-1 (pbk.: alk. paper)

DEDICATED
TO
ALLEN GINSBERG

ACKNOWLEDGMENTS

Most of these poems, in different versions, first appeared in the following publications, to which grateful acknowledgment is made: *Alpha Beat Soup, The Beat Book, The Beat Journey, The Beat Vision, The Columbia Review, The D.H. Lawrence Review, Epoch, Exquisite Corpse* (L.S.U.), *Greensboro Review, Grinning Idiot, Harper's, Homage to Henry, The Kerouac Connection, The Limberlost Review, Longhouse, Moody Street Irregulars, New & Experimental Writing, New Letters, New Mexico Quarterly Review, Our Poets Workshop, Palantir, Partisan Review, Poetry Magazine* (Chicago), *Poetry Northwest, Poetry NOW, Sarcophagus, The Southern Review, Staten Island Review, Texas Review, Voices, Wake, Western Review,* and in the chapbooks, *The Bowling Green Poems* (unspeakable visions of the individual press—1977), *Death Drag* (The Limberlost Press—1979), and *Dire Coasts* (The Limberlost Press—1987–1988).

MUSE WOOING: A SONG

Strangeness, come again
    like a special girl
        into the afternoon loft.
Strangeness, bentness, interest,
    come again to me with the quirk
        of my special mind.
Strangeness, I'll woo you as one should
    who's done with flirting.
I'll wait the mood of the sax,
    the salts of day, paprika-nights—
        waiting to be honored one more time.
But strangeness of heart,
        come again.

CONTENTS

Early Poems

Later Poems

NIGHT
MUSIC

EARLY POEMS

1946–1952

Our sole addition to the tenor of the times—
We'd come to Belsen armed with Henry James.

Fear in the Afternoon

Watched and sleeping all the sodden afternoon,
Listened until the creeping song began to moan
And sleeping stealthy sang along but did not mean.

And the slow blinds so drawn against the sun,
Or the sly yawn that signifies one's really sane,
And the clouds that fawn on sky and gather soon.

All this blots out the ancient ruined wall,
The twilight flute, the incense, and the Druid wail,
And this is Now, and all, though final, still is well.

—1946

Obituary for Jan Masaryk

Another conscience leaps from a window sill,
another statesman of this stateless world
is dead upon the stones
he knew would silence if they failed to kill.
A flagless era's funeral flags unfurl,
newspapers praise his bones,
and commissariats yawn
at talk of murder; pride
is mourned as suicide,
and only Thomists care where he has gone.

The news-morgue photos tomb his troubled face,
laying a filial wreath to finally unhex
his father and this time.
The stones and simple gravity erase
those eyes that glimmered in the Rolleiflex,
now freeze-framed in self-crime.
A decent man's outrage—
his sense of what is good
(helpless, in solitude)—
steps to the sill and leaps free of our age.

The broken body has no martyrdom.
The ghoulish eulogies provide that later.
But some nobility
is there. French Louis when the Terror came
believed at the knife, amidst ill-mannered laughter,

his own civility.
This man believed the saws
Versailles had overstated,
and those who find them dated
wager a winding-sheet with History's daws.

Now there are flowers on his nation's grave—
political wreaths as private people grieve.
The public men are massing
all their legions. Those more subtly alive
glimpse in his refusal to survive
another code that's passing.
Another blind man falls,
who could not bear this time's
unjudged, unpunished crimes,
or live without the tree beyond the walls.

Now he has leapt beyond the walls to death,
knowing the tree will wither, droop, and fall,
when Dialectics come—
knowing, as well, that every nation's wreath
is cut from one taproot sustaining all.
Still, his surrender numbs—
a whiplash to the bone;
his way of staying true
to ethics that the New
Mediaevalism thrusts from sill to stone.

—1948

DOCTOR TRUSTUS:
MAN OF GOOD WILL

"Grey is the color of all theory . . . "
—Goethe

I fumbled with my oldish books last night,
read Aristotle, Spencer and Montaigne,
gave partial due to Marx and Thomas Paine,
and frowned on Lucian in the frowning light.
Spinoza cast his obvious skill on me
and Darwin bored me with his formulae.
But dialectic, faith and vertebrae
had lost their magic and geometry.
I wrote a paper on our heritage
but stumbled with the grammar. Then I grieved
for all the nonsenses we once believed
that are forgotten in this witless age.

I gave it up, the paper and the grammar,
sadly put all the oldish books away,
arranged my desk to do reviews today,
tried to correct my intellectual stammer.
But Lucian whispered all ideas are false,
and Montaigne said be old and true;
Spinoza added One and Man as two,
while Spencer played the drum for Darwin's waltz.
Karl Marx defined the evils of our cage
and Aristotle laughed and Paine was peeved.
And all the nonsenses I once believed
were like the frothings of a rabic sage.

I fumble with my newish books tonight,
with Lenin, Kierkegaard and Jung and Freud.
With Spengler I am scared, with Sartre annoyed
and Ebbing makes my love of silks take flight.
Lenin dissects my home and Kierkegaard
rejects my soul, while Jung inspects my mind.
My home is built of hours; my soul, I find,
of bile; my easy thoughts are really hard.
A paragraph by Krafft becomes a page
in Freud; and Spengler says that he's perceived
decay, while Sartre finds everyone deceived . . .
And all my oldish books are not a gauge.

The doctors of the grey medicinal couch
say sex, once shocking to the freest prude,
is not a riddle but a platitude.
Pinching an ego makes it utter "ouch."
Reading, I cannot find the arguments
that once enticed us to the righteous kill—
that old determinism and free will
we loved till we found neither had much sense;
Or economics and the class-outrage,
and metaphysics through my desk perceived;
and all the nonsenses that we believed
that now are hurried off the empty stage.

The jealousies of has-been absolutes
carve up the lines. They steal each other's scenes
and stop the play with Ends embracing Means,
encircled and reduced by squaring Roots.
And now the curtain's down and by the light
I see the dying Men of Goodish Will
who have ideals and punish those who kill,

speaking humanities in the lowering night—
who cannot see the cross-bars for the cage.
And then—it was the hour—then I perceived
myself amid those nonsenses deceived
in faith by this, a grey and heretic age.

—1948

LES ITALIENNES

—for Marian in a line of Pound's

In our bed you offer me your maid
as though I were obese and you'd delude
me in my satiation, feed me food
sweetened enough to frustrate, not dissuade.
You have denied me, sent a shadow breast
for me to feast on, lips to close my lips
with servant kisses from which duty slips
to save her mistress from a vague unrest.
Your mouth that speaking is as soft as ore,
torn in the mining, now is hard as sense.
Your motion slows to wench's indolence
as though "you" watched and giggled from the door.
Oh, you are rare and dark as art who touch me—
what curious shame would your denial teach me?

—1948

9

Instructions for the World Librarian

—after John Donne

When this grave's mould is broken up again—
whatever reason your new times may find—
let any ghoul or statistician then
dismiss the lines of our age that was blind,
    but not with innocence;
blind in the brutal, frightened way of wolves
    who turn upon themselves
when all the burning brush becomes a fence.
But let those geiger-guarded people hear
these meditative words that see too clear
behind Aurelius' sentiment, his fear.

If they come from a land or out of times
when no one needs to justify their lives,
our thoughts will seem the mortar joining rhymes,
our words atonal and our fears the knives
    in paranoiac brains;
the poems of some subtle, nascent tongue
    that would corrupt the young
whose antiseptic culture knows no stains.
And when the world's made one by neutral 'trodes
they may, for fun, adopt these anguished modes
even as we kept our Horatian odes.

Firstly, we truly wanted love and faith
but sought them with leper's disbelief
in cures. We tried them all, desiring truth

10

to prove us wrong and give us some relief.
    For love and peace were fables
in an age of many nice-told tales,
    and all were fictional.
We stamped our ills with deft Homeric labels
but never saw, for safety was the prize,
that myths seen to be myths by hopeful eyes
and still repeated guiltily, are lies.

If you have got a sane and dull age, burn
these relics lest they bear our rabic doubt
upon them, like some radio-active fern
that is so green and wet to feel without
    the clean, untactile glove.
Remember all precautions when you touch
    us, for we are much
like fishes dying in the spasmic act of love.
And all that are bored or rebel on your globe
keep from these words of one who had no robe
but felt himself a masochistic Job.

—*1948*

NIGHT MUSIC

Do not be afraid
though the light is far.
Dawn has been delayed
on another star.
Though it's very far,
do not be afraid.

The unrepentant vein
consummates the past.
In the dark and rain
the future's falling fast:
consummate the past,
O unrepentant vein.

Though we've been unmade,
care will speak to care.
Hope has been betrayed,
nothing else is sure.
But care will speak to care
when we've been unmade.

Though the dream is fast
in a night of rain,
dreams can be amassed
where the night has lain.
In a ceaseless rain
only dreams are fast.

Lip on lip is laid,
rest and rest secure.
Impure men are made,
love is always pure.
Rest, and rest secure:
lip on lip is laid.

Love alone will last,
love is what we are.
In it, we are cast;
night can never mar
what we really are.
Love alone will last.

Do not be afraid
in a night of rain.
The unrepentant vein
rests, and rests secure.
Though we've been unmade,
love is what we are.

Though the light is far
and the dream is fast,
consummate the past.
Lip on lip is laid,
care will speak to care,
love alone will last.

—*1950*

The Memoirs of
an Imaginary Man

"That morning we discovered the patient
crouching in a jar. He was fairly well
preserved . . .

—Doktor Krafft in *Caput Mortuum*

Another starless night, another novel;
outside the city rustles with the rain.
This is the hour I probe an author's navel
or let a poet list his latest pain;
and ladle down the windiest of drivel
and try to lie where famous men have lain.
Tonight the stars have organized a claque
to cheer a God who's never coming back.

More bored than I could possibly describe
(the weightless silence threatens to consume),
I scrawl upon this paper like a crab
who is less horrible than he must seem;
complete a sentence and begin to scrub
the words away, which darken all the same,
and will not be erased. Instead *I* fade,
as though I was a thing that they had made.

When young I had the infant's fancy habits.
Believing calmly no one else existed,
I fashioned people like so many rabbits,
a sure supply of love to be exhausted.
Mother was allowed to live and kibbitz
but all the others vanished when I fasted.
To talk to me could be a great ordeal
as I was quite abnormally unreal.

One day an unseen friend went up in flames;
I hid the matches and refused to tell.
I horrified my father, sucking limes,
believing they would keep me two feet tall.
I kept a scrapbook of my life and times:
a leaf, some nails, a word I couldn't spell,
a penknife name of Bill, a flattened ball,
drawings of angels, nudes, a corpse, a wall.

I grew to manhood like a paper flower
that has no roots and blossoms at the touch
of water in a bowl, and lives an hour.
What grace I had was ironed in with starch,
I did my meditating in the shower,
and changed my concepts promptly every March.
I scoffed at Christmas, but believed in Scrooge:
my dream-collection was, by this time, huge.

I had the usual affairs, I played
at sex as though it was a human chess.
My talk was witty, I would never plead
but practiced with a mirror, saying "yes."
I managed to keep pretty well employed
but used another name, a false address.
The Juliets found me thrillingly adult;
the Cleopatras liked the cards I dealt.

I hid behind elaborate attitudes
and gave to each a sort of grisly style.
I got a wart from handling phantom toads:
it made a funny story for a while.
I drowned a woman's spaniel in the tides
and acted modest when it made her vile.
I managed to be interesting and chase her,
but now a sentence mocks at my eraser:

"I have grown weary of my *Self* tonight—"
It stares at me, refusing to believe
that I am something human, though inert.
Somehow I need to see it to be live
because I am the thing the words denote,
and only reading them can I survive.
As unsubstantial as the heat in coal,
I am the music in a piano roll.

The clock electrically propels the hours
(I dare not look for fear that I will vanish).
The noises in the street create my ears;
my senses spread about the room like varnish
and have their life as long as nothing errs
in that perception of the words I furnish.
The self I wearied of, now in the ink,
will be obliterated if I blink.

I have a moment now and can compare—
before the bulb, whose idea is the light,
goes out and I'm dispersed into the air—
an instant to remember and relate
the *aegri somnia* of the affair.
The light is failing, it is very late;
the past is too uncertain to discharge,
the things I'd swear by few, the dream too large.

I tried to press my life in several books
and give to everything a sense of mission.
I was convinced that sex was good on bikes
and going to the john involved volition.
I filled the Bible's margins with rebukes
and made a riddle that defied solution.
I supplemented all my meals with rice,
and thought that mastication was a vice.

I visited my tailor's for a goiter
and knew that Isis was a summer drink.
I had my mother bound in alligator
and used to throw her ostrich eggs while drunk.
I wrote a verse, *The Vision in the Gutter,*
and always dropped my trousers when I drank.
I liked to state that breathing was the bunk
and tried to cash a menu in a bank.

My life, a series of symbolic actions
the aim of which has somehow slipped my mind,
was furnished with the gaudiest abstractions.
The date of my senses was designed
for computation in transfinite fractions—
the mettle of my soul was most refined.
I can't recall the first time I was able
to interchange a waiter and a table.

The trouble started when that wooden waiter
would not become a table that could speak.
I tried to make a man of Walter Pater
but he retained his feathers and his beak.
Than what I thought, I knew it was much later,
when looking in my glass I saw a geek.
I sat, as I sit now, as for a tryst.
And wait a Satan I know can't exist.

Certainly my heart knew semaphore
but always sent its messages in prose.
It was not capable of reaching far
but grew most urgent in request for praise.
Afflicted by unreason like catarrh,
I felt a perfect yearning to amaze,
forgetting that immense de Sade of urge
that man is Masoch to in every age.

. . . They've just instructed me to douse the light.
But don't they know what that will mean?
"I have grown weary of my *Self* tonight—"
And one must see to have one's self be seen.
I wrote down all of it that I could write,
but have forgotten much that came between.
In just a moment all will be quite clear,
but first, my name . . . THE MS. BREAKS OFF HERE.

—*1951*

PETITION CONCERNING THE DEATH-WISH

God of the World, all dread things suddenly make
as harmless to our life as tears at school;
uncoil the rope, deracinate the snake—
reveal him as a yawning, lovely fool.
Then dredge the danger from the brackish pool
and show it shallow, lilied and opaque.
Remove the fatal glitter from the tool,
and when we dream of falling let us wake.
For all our mortal world has got so cruel
that we are constantly afraid we'll break
our anxious image staring from the lake:
bring all these natural things beneath Your Rule.
Convince us there is nothing sure at stake.
Give back to us a safety to forsake.

—*1951*

THE SURVIVORS

—for Elga

Escape had gravely dulled our gear;
limping free, we sought our kind.
Guised in flesh to hide our fear,
age and world oppressed the mind.

Guilt made watchers on a star;
angels, guarding us, were blind;
loneliness had been unkind;
everywhere was dark and far.

Leaving innocence behind,
endeavoring to persevere,
alone, responsible, resigned,
grief lay carnally with fear.

Age-old urges, intertwined,
generated blinding fire.
Elijah knew, upon his pyre,
love is eyeless, but not blind.

Everywhere, so dark and far,
love is eyeless, but not blind;
grief is lying down with fear,
age and world oppress the mind.

—1951

WATCHING MORNING IN

—for Shirley

Look to the star that warns the morning in;
others have been in love before this day.
Darkness has been kicked back by other lovers
under that star, who watched the morning in.
Ours was a narrow craving yesterday;
now the fraternity of outlawed lovers,
meeting from evening out till morning in,
numbers our members. Now with the guilt of day,
we have become conspirators and lovers.

Agents of that belief that must await
the utmost night and fever to appear,
lovers proclaim in whispers and in flesh
the urge for safety for which all worlds wait,
the spirit's lunge beyond what things appear,
that flash of order struck by flesh on flesh.
For love is how we learn, if we must wait
a more extraordinary dark, to peer
into the open city of the flesh.

Lie just a moment then within our warmth . . .
The ebb and drowse of sleep reveals the world
this day will place around us and our love.
There will be little wonder, slender warmth—
lovers have small love left to give the world,
and only the loveless make a law of love.
But for a moment more of dozing warmth

let us indulge this vision of the world,
the one illusion natural to love:

That watching morning in, the world would wait;
the separate terrors disappear; the day
prove kind to lovers, who renew in flesh
that warmth that could undo the world, that love.

—1952

LATER POEMS
1959–1988

Walk like a heron, swim like a fish.
Whatever moves, moves through everything.

Too-Late Words to my Father
(1899–1959)

i

Camden nights dire with honeysuckle,
back of hospital streets,
stoops murmurous with baseball—
Sucking peppermints in an alien town,
I carried plastic tubes of sleeping pills,
aspirin, iodine, and oil of camphor—
prepared against myself but ill-prepared for vigils
in South Jersey shipyard Whitman night,
      or the irony of turnpike smashup
        that brought you there,
          my urbane father.

Scotches in Bruno's across the street at nine,
watching, as I do, the drinkers at the bar,
the television-starers, the pinball athletes,
the beehived waitresses—mothers mostly—
who like to serve hot food to men.
Wore the same suit a week, my only suit,
      and watched till midnight in your room
        the waning flickers
          of mortality.

ii

The Pemigewasset Hotel Bar in angry thirties,
worsening towards amity in Munich,
went away from me this summer.
Guy Lombardo, golf clubs, ravelling gentility,
New York Times on French toast-Sunday
(you pared your nails at noon precisely
and I bite mine still)—all went away.
No credo from your life kept you alive in Camden—
tenacity mysterious and unsuspected.
Beloved enemy, more beleaguered than I knew,
      more flesh courage than I knew,
          no *idea* of courage,
             went away.

After thrombosis, your meager leg, the good one left,
lifted from habit at the weight of blankets.
They tried to filch your teeth to clean them,
though I was positive they were your own,
your eyes uprolling like a paw-trapped bear's
as student nurses, giggling, vied
to get their fingers in your mouth—
a choreography of slapstick dentists.
I fed you invalid hospital custards,
tickled your deadened foot to get response,
and would have eased you if I could.
        I left a light turned on for you to see
           your way back home
              to 1914.

All that I know is useless—
fathers doomed to bafflement at sight
of their myopic sons with time to burn;

sons orphaned in the heart before the fact—
       Missed chances as sour in the mouth
         as mornings of remembered
           pettiness.

Anyway, you were fastidious in your broken bed,
tried to control your bowels, wipe your mouth.
A Negro nurser sobbed to see you stare,
unable to swallow, at God's face
as she invoked His intercession.
You made contacts even among bedpan carriers—
       more than I could do with my enormous glasses,
         fogged with memory's montage
           of dada imagery.

Now you won't read to me again
though I write stories and this poem
because you read me Dickens before sleep—
Marley so utterly dead in your American voice,
deader than you've become.
From you, I caught a taste for language,
never to confess it in our wrangles.
       Though proud of me, the use I put it to
         left the Jeffrey Farnol in you
           speechless.

Did you get back to the boy's-book world
before flu epidemics, prep schools, Miss Florence
(our common dancing teacher) to the amber
Teddy Roosevelt days of knickered certainty?
Did you finally streak around the Dartmouth's end,
a reedy, high-strung quarterback for Williams?
What happened to the straw-hat you doffed—
a gallant on the pier—when, undivorced,
we landed back from California in 1931?

You dressed deftly, charmed children, knew names,
and loved all women like a precocious youth
witched by an English teacher's ankle.
Though you were never sure, they loved you too.
All your wives, your jobs, your maddening cars!
      The mind of the rememberer escapes,
          like Ishmael,
            to tell.

iii

Somehow can't swallow your loss though—
my stomach throws it up with breakfast.
Latterly, we shared a few bad hangovers
(weakness is a bond), sipped morning beers
to unthrob heads earned trying to get along,
waded the seaweed tidelines of Peconic to dive deep
where all was tranquil as the past should be.
I'll never smell a Camel without recalling you,
and didn't cry for you until you lost your hand—
then chiefly at the horror of dismemberment you'd feel.
You never knew I waited there those nights in Camden,
some veil already masked your eyes,
but I was the troubled stranger, who sat still,
smoking too much and praying his mouth's God
that you'd escape the last despair,
      knowing his generation's helplessness to succor
         sentience most valued
           when most lost.

iv

But these plain words are truer than the ornate ones
said over you in the expensive box
(I picked the suit you wore, knowing your tastes)
in banks of plastic lilies, silly daffodils,
and hotel-friends from Cincinnati.
One woman leaned and touched your bloodless arm—
horrible affectation of false grief, it seemed.
But then perhaps you'd touched her once—
winning, importunate, a little drunk—
                and still this side of pleasure
                        willing to risk
                            remorse.

The room was stifling with other people's faiths—
you'd lived faithless, run too fast to ponder.
The Holmes'-contentiousness roiled on
even in the presence of your husk
sleeping in an attitude unlike you—calm, indrawn.
The old Peconic people, the Family, were there,
having survived the boisterous nephew,
cousin, uncle, son—into his silenced world.
Your mother waited in another room, no words for her,
you clear in her eyes, fourteen, a worry still,
never to burrow into her lap again, cajoling love,
                never to be sure you had it—
                    though she was sure
                        where you had gone.

Lost Jamaica funeral wastelands of dead August,
jukebox bars down heat-stunned boulevards,
grieving Midwesterners, easier to tear than us.
Sixty years of mornings end in an afternoon.

I didn't look around on leaving;
what I had to say came later—now.
Gesturing outwards all your life,
you knew the names of seven hundred salesmen,
and the boy who sat in front of you in 1910.
An empty garrulousness, I'd always thought.
And yet in that way you cut closer to the bone
than both your gifted brothers.
                Your God was in Chicago and New York
                        and some few cities
                                in between.

            v

So, oh, your thin Camden legs under the sheet,
your thin fleet meatless legs learning
something new to do in bed at sixty.
You didn't seem afraid of the conclusive night ahead,
stared quizzically at your bandaged stump,
keeping in life that way, and sometimes
looked at me out of your oxygen-dark
wondering who it was sat up so long with you.
I talked on with awful pointlessness,
embarrassed by my breaking voice.
But I spoke out of time and its ego—
the shame of something-more-to-lose—

                    And end this now,
                        become your son
                            at last.

                                —1959–1973

                        30

MOUTH

I am all mouth,
must have it filled,
made to swallow everything—
It is when it is no longer
excess of hunger—
It is when this changes
from seeking the Other
to devouring Otherness—
It is when I want to eat
rather than taste—
when I wish to consume
rather than gently lick—
It is when I am nothing
but the Great Mouth
rather than the Great Hunger—
that I know I am losing myself,
my eye-teeth grown dangerous,
capable of masticating life—

out of despair of capture,
   and the insatiable mouth
      in my mind.

—1961

WOMEN IN A.M.

Women drowse through mornings, nurturing life.
Some women never rouse except by twilight.
They save the real expenditures for dark.
Drowsing in dream-peopled beds,
no anguish in their mornings,
only the flesh-warm linen,
the whish of rain, the soul at sleep.
They are ingathering, they are in root,
and I'm unhappy to be up and writing it.

—1961

Premonitory July

After the flood or fire or deadly cloud—
whatever it will be this final time—
if anything comes back, little animals will—
to go about the natural business of what's left.

We can't last forever in our blinkered pride,
our hard eyes and abstract words
in which no hint of humility in the face
of nature remains, no residue at all.

But little chipmunks will come back,
rabbits pausing like garden statuary,
nostrils whickering as in a trance;
all manner of birds and stoats and moles come back—
little creatures whose only counterfeitness
is a certain caution in our presence.

We can't last forever here, but grass will grow,
nuts fall, be gathered, grow, and fall again,
the true business of reality recommence
amid the vast irrelevance of our images.

But then it's too easy to be Chinese these days,
and they're all Western now—we're them.
Some sort of sad justice in that irony . . .
The death in us may die too late.

—1961

SADE ON CALVARY

1

Sade, misunderstood, went to jail
    for wanting to love Rose Keller
      with the only rod he had—
a victim of imagination's insatiety.
But is it really nobler to kill oneself—
    than the world which failed
      to evoke one's love?

2

Sade on Calvary: no women mourned
    though he was willing
    to take upon his flesh
the bitter contradictions of the mind.
At the eleventh hour, he groaned aloud,
    having the last orgasm,
and died in expiation of our virtues,
    leaving us that bravery to revile
    without which cowards are uneasy.

—1963

COLD WINDOW

Crow pecking a patch of last ice—
    live beak against the wind's knife.
Shabby firs,
    grass without nutrients,
    nothing behind the dead sky.
No God
      or atheist certainty.

I am a man to the crow
    as he is a crow to me—
    though I am watched from no window.
Eye frozen by distance,
    empty circle only love could fill—
But damn the metaphor.

Cigarettes,
    ten in the morning,
      Equinil—
and years to go before wisdom.
Spring brings birds back,
    grass distills its green,
    skies lift with godhead
        despite incertitude.

Still, winter wants a bitter word in passing.

—1963

THE VOCATION

This riot, this obsession, this preoccupation—
    suddenly age has edged my eye.
I hear something coming towards me,
I have reached mid-point without a voice,
I sit writing and writing in a book.
    A hard word—
    a sinewy thought—
    a single image!
I sit writing about them in another book.

—1964

A Bad Turn

High, burnished sky,
the snow squall roars off south
over the Sound in a huge reef—

I ginger my car across the river bridge
having driven a blizzard in Nebraska once.
Mulling old failures, I take no notice,
Nebraska and Connecticut no different—
like these flat words.

Yeats wasn't good till forty,
not yet himself—

But I am sick of counting other men's dates
on bitten fingernails.

So many snow squalls moving away
over a stalled life.

—1964

YEAR'S END

In the quiet, in the snow,
this Sunday before Christmas,
tired and diligent too long,
a knot in the heart relents.

I think of the gypsies of the Var,
who have been "out" for centuries,
and of their greasy pots and flivvers—
and there is a longing for tribes again,
for human units familial enough
for the affections to enclose.

So I have my company on my walls.
Alone, a man must have the thought
of spirits sympathetic to his work.
But something is broken—
I am not the same as I was before.
Some armature is broken.

I am glad I was serious enough
        to be broken.

                              —1964

STATEMENTS IN A
PERSONAL WINTER

—after Rimbaud

Disruption has become my secret cause.
I age without grace, a cold freedom achieved.
Anarchy—a city of blind windows.
I want to be elsewhere, a stranger down the bar.
I should have the guile to quit while losing.
Whatever blessing comes will come too late.
When I was young I loved the world too much.
Now my spirit is as sour as vinegar.
Longing has worn me down to a blunt axe.
This torture has its trump in a cough.
Twitter, twitter until midnight comes.
But better silence. Better silence and snow.

—1965

MIDNIGHT OIL

Still up at midnight, addled,
    I'm bewildered, being alone this way.
The muffled TV keeps me company,
    the sleeper near me restive with a dream,
    excluding me farther, out of reach,
I am bewildered to find myself here and now—
        it seems unlikely.
I try to imagine someone who would
    stay up, insomniac, with me.

I can come up with no one real—
    only phantoms of lonesomeness.
Peopling the ticking dark, they empty it.
    I am bewildered, I am calm, I puzzle it,
        not understanding.
Nothing to do after that but will-to-sleep.
    At least the deadened hours
    promise dawn and irony.

—1965

UNWANTED 1943
CHAPPAQUA FLASHBACK

All at once remembering the copses and hills
of Westchester, still country then,
when I was seventeen, and still integral too,
      the uprush of spring in me.
When you are young and opened-out
the world enlarges Self to a wider eye—
      the days are long enough,
      you breathe by older rhythms,
      not to unsmiling clocks.
The wonder of it, the dawn-drenched lawns
    when I, alone in that valley, walked,
    the dog loyally with me in the newness.
      I felt charged with light.
      It was the last time I believed.
Come into my manhood, all doubts ahead,
    I was drunk with certainties.
    I was a poet, wings of the morning!
How I loved, and longed for love, and walked
      as naturally as the dog ran.
The sunny breakfast-room after my wanderings;
    the virgin joys of day, a feast
    for all my green absorptions.
It was the last magic of my youth—
    before I learned that magic's
        incommunicable.
It was enough then to be within it,
I wanted for nothing, I was complete,

my mouth was sweet and wet.
And autumn had its smoky aura too—
the early twilights,
sex in an armchair,
her limbs flung open to the fire's flicker,
me fumy with a tyro's forming hopes—
All, all perishing and it felt immortal.

O, there was time
and one was discovering,
and nothing was cruel or unchangeable or forever.
One gloomed about death—
Housman and Lawrence—
but one's flesh was alien to the idea,
one only played the fancy's house in it.
Indian-leafed hillsides
(spring's freshet having
flooded into summer's pond)
now, in sere autumn, the soul fermenting—
dark, thick, rare, distilled by August noons.
No premonitions,
only stiffer winds—
the chilly winds that rise at five o'clock
in an October one made Poe-esque then—
there seemed to be a way to pluck romance from anything.

I remember now in the rueful way
of remembering wonder when one
has less wonder left,
knowing it is better to be a foolish, rapt young poet,
"knowing" nothing, than to be
a serious writing man, recalling it,
worrying the words,
trying to be accurate,
measuring Self against three decades' leveling gales.

Having learned to live with death
　　　　　as with an old wife,
　　　　　the struggle over,
　　　the bickerings over with at last,
　　　　　burdened with maturity,
　　　　　able to forebear,
not proud of compromise but prisoned in it,
　　　　　no longer fevering.
Nevertheless I know that loss of the sap of life
　　　　　that is the little death—
　　　so fleeting, so ephemeral, no return.

I am silenced with an armisticed-fatality,
　　　　　unmanned, blank-eyed as a fish,
wrenched backwards to a phantom-time—
　　　lost along with all its ignorant grace.
As if I had rowed out too far, had drifted.
Nothing so sobering and lonely as an abandoned dory
　　　pulled towards an unwatched foundering
　　　　　in the coldly westering light
　　　　　　　over a November sea.
Yet I must row, and bail, and, yes, recall—
　　　　　I dare do nothing less.

—1968

43

The Suzy Q

—for Susan

Your unbruised eyes over the hurt mouth
looking from an awful distance—

I never lay with that other girl in you,
only saw her level eyes hankering out—

Short linen kimona, black French tights
in a one-room, cat-shit corner of the city,
shadeless, a single eerie bulb, us finally nude—

Second time drunk that day,
I sobered over your girl's body laid out
inert as a cadaver on the bed,

and gave up on myself, emptied by pity,
urgent to give you back your own completeness,
to awaken a little vanity in those eyes.

Perhaps succeeded for half an hour.

Never saw you again to be sure.

—1968

DYING LAWRENCE

The mean deaths of the spirit in this age—
the era's only nobility guttering out
        around cafe tables,
        in second-class coaches,
        on hired beds—
Poets in bank clerk's bodies, self-consumed.

And so the urge to write about Lawrence.
    Not *to* him, he is nothing now.
But about his eyes in Bandol
        badgered by vulgarity—
behind geranium shutters
    glimpsing whatever future
we ravaged consciousnesses have.
The busy dogs of Bandol
    knew he was intensely among them,
his high pitch of conscious life
        burning, and burning up.
No longer any way to shutter down the eye.
The burden of spring's recurrence,
        its remorseless fecundity
        indifferent to his fever—
he coughed against the knowledge
that each year pomegranates swell new.

What broke Lawrence
    was what he saw
at the bottom of the garden.

Half-a-man with his narrow face,
charred sticks of walking bone,
the quick of movement finally blurred,
the fierce, unveiling eyes—
        spaniel's eyes—
cornered at last.
        Self-exiled from Albion,
and further exiled by his prescience,
an oceanic longing—for death's fathoms—
        rose in his wren's chest.
A fearful bliss swelled up in him
    at the imminent mystery—
        life's consummation,
        the bridal night to come.

To be quite blotted out—
    taken back into the flow—
re-wombed in oblivion.

I ponder again his difficult passage out,
    his foot in Frieda's hands,
a dog yapping somewhere up the street in Venice,
and death bringing the huge blue silence
        like ceremonial gentians
            to the bon voyage,
leaving primroses on England's hedges,
        and a sense of absence—
            a fissure in the time—
                an empty berth.

Lord, how meager some men make the flesh.

                    —*1968*

DECLINE OF THE WEST

Ours was a short day,
dawn rushing on noon
like a film speeded past a lens.
And then a blandish afternoon,
smoke swimming up through flicker,
the brief chill of October twilight
clearing the eye to the darkness
gathering beyond the streetlamps.
All this felt in Florence for a certainty—
rich autumn lapsing in a spectral city.

Remembering the antic crowds
in grainy newsreels
we knew were decades dead.

—1968

Berryman's Dead

The most important happening
    in the world today:
old "Henry's" off the bridge.
I hope he had cancer, or was drunk,
        or the young wife gave up on him—
I hope against everything I know.
To live in a world unlivable to poets—
        harder every day.

Morning comes with the nausea
    of elegies yet unwritten.
His magpie-eloquence went to water.
    He stilled himself, jumped free.
We're left here at the rail
    he railed about.

Bitterness, irony, tears—
The day come down again
        to Alas.

—*1972*

DEATH DRAG
(THE ELEGIST)

The poet, tagged by bourbon,
collects his maggoty imagery
to tool on schedule another keen—
bitter as Brecht with bitterness
at years of swallowing a boy's sob
to write a man's memoriams.

The tides inhale/exhale the cove—
a dying planet's saline respiration;
night ebbs and dawn floods back
as hope once flooded in the boy—
avid for life in Dachau's time.

Smoke shrouds the elegist,
his teacup fills with coffin-nails.
He hammers out four lines
as hollow as the empty space
a murdered friend has left.

The poet, sick to death of death,
aging without grace, gone to Haydn,
strives to achieve the easy tears of Li Tai Po,
who threw his griefs in the cold Yangtze,
then boiled the supper rice.

—*1973*

49

CHINESE POETS

Clouds stand lordly over Fenwick
in September air, lucid as water.
Distant sounds of hammering,
summer houses closing up.
I walk my old three-miler
to the lighthouse and the esplanade
as clouds of wrens erupt
from lavender reeds, tall as me.

I mend from last week's poisons—
a middle-aged man making resolutions—
as Tu Fu opens the clenched throat
to the actual, suspirant world.
I note new houses, a floppy awning
for a canceled dance, golf-carts,
men watering the billiard greens,
bluejays vagrant as gulls far out.

Chu Wan said a thousand years ago:
"The Empire of Ch'in has passed away."
My belly eases with this knowledge.

Walk like a heron, swim like a fish.
Whatever moves, moves through everything.

—*1973*

Writing the Atheneum talk, I wonder—
How can I bring it back?
The Cedar Bar in 1957,
San Remo illuminations earlier,
Jack on the Minetta curb
prophesying *Doctor Sax*—

Here, in the mud, eating sausages at dawn,
I ransack memory in history's name,
calling back that irretrievable excitement—the drunk
lucidities of brash young men.

A beer-bottle, shattered in the street,
broke Jack's vision into laughter.
But dawn, edging down MacDougall,
promised more poems after sleep.
We knew, though muzzily, what we knew.

Now smokes and booze have thrust the body,
like a spike, into the tireless mind,
and hope, a spinning tire, into the mud.
But still that laughter gets me out of bed
to make a public gesture
to those shards of glass,
that street of squalid walk-ups
silvered by our thought.

Now those certainties have all the charm
   of boyhood's notes to God
   returned to sender—

A calico cat foraging a doom of garbage cans.

                    —*1975*

FOR WALKER EVANS

Walker dead now—
    Urge to words,
but sick of writing death-poems:
        Berryman's poem to Roethke dead,
        Lowell's poem to Berryman.
        Sexton's poem to Plath dead,
        my poem to Sexton—
Sops backed up in a stuck sink.
Walker succumbed
        to busted plumbing
            in his 70s.
Still, one quick intelligence less—
the bird-bright eye under the ground.

Who'll ever see Bethlehem, P.A., the same?

—1975

Weekend Away

And if there can be love again
                between such wearied people
there can be oysters
                smiling in their shells,
            Franz Kline, cold marts, bouzouki music.
There can be night's laughter on Atheneum Square
            and dawns with an end in sight—
return of the old sensual fevers
            resting the expended parts of us.
            So life's got savor now—
                there's grace in it.

For if there can be flesh-love again
            between bodies so self-haunted—
            hand-colloquies in hotel-beds,
            words become tongues—
in time there could be all the rest,
memory proven tougher than despair,
            an end of soldiering-through.

I kissed you in the marriage-places,
                grounded again.
There's nothing more to lose.
            The old Zen canniness occurred—
mountains were mountains once again.

                                —*1975*

54

Work on in the faith
        that the corner will be turned.
Without a god, that's got to be
                the faith.
Accept it without further speculation
as a Catholic accepts the Eucharist.
If art's the last religion
        be a trusting and obedient
                communicant.
Perform its rituals
in simple hope of heaven—
        work down through the circles
        towards new light.

                —*1975*

Fayetteville Dawn (1)

Now cocks crow coop to coop
    over cicada-buzz
    bird-cheep
    and katydid
across the ragged pastures
    still noon warm
this hour before dawn.

Without the sounds of our machinery
    air-conditioners off
    radios asleep
    no snores
here in an apartment complex
    on the edge of town
you hear this hubbub going on

of things with wings
recharging for the day

preparing to wait out our noise again.

    —1975

Storm in the Ozarks

Northward, the black sky at dusk
    heaps up, evil with lightning,
    blacker than the idea of tomorrow.
Trees gone abject, leaves bellied up,
that sky comes on us avalanche-slow,
and Shirley notes the monster-shape—
    old bogey of her Southern girlhood—
and wants to crawl beneath the double bed
as I, the outlander, exult,
    "Adventure! Marvelous!"

She draws the drapes against the gale,
    premonitory onrush torturing
    the double-trunked mimosa,
        savior-tree.
Of a sudden, it is easy
to believe in weather-gods
    to whom our existence
    has no consequence.
Bolts of lightning crackle like barrage,
thunder dooms my teleologies,
huge splats of rain beat daisies flat,
the eyeball feels the tearing strain
    where branch and tree trunk join.
An old primordial fatalism
    wipes out an existential century
    and its umbrellas in a flash.

The farmer-in-the-senses
　　puts his rakes away
　　and thinks of cellars
　　　　as the urban voice repeats,
　　　　"Adventure! Marvelous!"
But the wiser roots of the mimosa
grip red clay and buried stone
　　　　as the unheeding avalanche of wind
　　　　arrives at some blind behest.

And ruin is our future,
that good ruin that reminds
our sentience that death's
　　　　as natural as breath;
visceral fright rousing respect
　　　　in a respectless time,
glimpse of life's impersonality
in which we are less rooted
　　　　than the huge mimosa,
　　　　　　fallen.

The daisies will come back.

Marvel on that, adventurer.

—1975

Fayetteville Dawn (2)

Nail-paring moon in winter sky
    through etch of twig,
and I feel close to Snyder—
my image in the night-window,
the pangs drowned in bourbon,
      history still dogging me.
I have achieved an isolation
too absolute for lonesomeness.
That leaves me with the breathing world,
      an exit from Self attainable
    after these years of fret,
the beauty-ungraspable in reach at last,
the footprint-moon raked clean
      in the rinsed lens of eye.
So we can die out of time, and sleep
      to wake new perhaps.
What's happened to the moon?
Quenched in coffee-dregs.

—1977

OUT OF A FEVER:
FOR ROBERT LOWELL
(SEPT. 13, 1977)

This is an age of elegy in our poetry.
He morning-aftered everyone from Ford to Berryman.
Now he's gone off in a cab (just as he used to do),
not to come back this time. Yet I can't feel the curses
of the young at death's fat yawn at seriousness,
just the illusion of the futility of our endeavors—
which is all that's left of youth in me.

An engineer of breath, a poet's fevers
burn on, year in, life out, until the
last expenditure's demanded—breath itself.

Maule's curse hung over him, and me—
exalte mothers, ne'er-do-wells for fathers,
Sunday roasts, linen stiff as board, awesome uncles,
dead leaves scuttling through a burying ground,
reviving stink of bilgy harbors after a carouse.
He got free with half his wits intact, and so did I.

His exemplary life caesuraed now—pacifist, poet,
teacher, inmate, drunk—a typical contemporary scribe.
Dogged by history, his attempts to leash it
were a True Believer's ethic in a beliefless age.
But what we'll miss next year will be his thorny line.

Cheating world, that woos a man's concern,
then kills him for his trouble with a grin—
But enough of that. This Holmes salutes that Lowell
on this day of his abrupt departure for Back Bay.

—*1977*

NORTHFORK OCTOBER RETURN

Sea-scut, bayberries, aquamarine,
northwest white-capped wind, ketch
beating up the Sound tight-reefed,
the shoals of bluefish running now:
he'd ventured back to these tidelines,
sea-weeded with old memories,
after the tumor of July, the radiation-August,
the long depression of September, and,
laboring his breath along,
irradiated to the last eyetooth,
impatient with prolonged recuperation,
haunted the beaches where the curse
or blessing took place long ago,
and waited out obsession with his wound—

Lost boyhood haven, still salt-worn
as cloudy bits of bottle glass,
was it for this I was preparing?
The dream of harbor swamped so fast
by chance gusts of an easterly?

Gas ached beneath his heart, he fought
assaults of panic, curdling to self-pity
the cove he'd hoped-for proven phantom,

befogged by all the buoyless drift
of his four decades' exile from this place—

Sea-sleep, he begged in secret, *come*
and ease my heart, kedge-anchored still
off Horton's Point with no way in.
Cold petrel spirit of these tides,
excuse me for a little, I was innocent
believed life's risks without a tab,
who now, an anxious, aging scold,
must make a final fight or bitter-over—
Scud this sprung dory to some berth.

The gulls persisted into stiffening wind,
coasting its shoals and currents in the sun
to Greenport's fish-rich jetties east.
He tried to find a long down-draft
to take him also out beyond
Peconic's headlands to the empty beach
where table-rocks were scored with 20s names.
And warred in silence the last giving-up,
the armistice of ultimate undertow.

Stay with me till I mend, you rocks,
the ragged teeth of that bedraggled
coast, *bear up a coward's weight*
until tomorrow's fresh with resolutions,
cheap tears turned as tough as brine.

The second morning there, it came
while he was blank, distracted—
a settling below the heart.

Amid the ebb-drained strew that dawn,
three fragile scallop shells,
chaste as their absent Venuses,
lay in his empty hand and eye.
He hunkered down, boyrapt, to ponder
their fluted edges perfect as the poem
already forming in the tide's return.

—*1982*

LAWRENCE IN TAOS

Dead as a doornail,
live as the wind,
a ghost-fox haunts the Taos hills—
savage scavenger,
crazed messiah,
unshriven spirit of the place—
Dare we comprehend the portent
of the carrion-moons he bayed down once?

—1984

DIRE COASTS

Stranded here in Ishmael's November
I'm longing for deep water, dire coasts,
our snaggle of rock beach,
the brine-trace in the air back there,
the feeble sweep of lighthouse beam
beaconing blind shipping in—
clearwater for a brackish man
whose mind's a swamp of words.

Looking for a Self outside self,
an end to ten years in these Ozarks
and loss of natural magnetic North.
A house near Greenport in the sand—
shingled, punished, proved by weather;
the graphic glare of forenoon
scouring a Hopper room,
a life's mucked decking holystoned
for final downwind tack to port;
a world of clams, Nor'westers,
mornings going somewhere;
a place appropriate to bargaining
with death, its demarcated clarities
come down to a lunar flood and ebb;
living by old frugalities,
appetites having achieved despair.

I want the crest and break of water,
I crave again the darker coves
I sailed in bilgy catboats once—
joyous, ignorant, sometimes brave—
but not for helm or halyard anymore,
only to walk beside, attuned
by widened pupils, nerves
alerted for minute connections,
senses poised for durable truths
hauled from the sea's impermanence—
to compass out last bearings there.

Here, I'm rudderless, adrift,
want nothing but the irreducible words—
symmetric, calcined, hard, their mystery
as eloquent and mute as bone—
so many oysters with a chance of pearls.

A rootless, aging man, imagining home.

—1985–1986

The Old Saybrook House

Our house resettles, waiting there
during this decade's long diaspora.
Our poignant summers only visits,
leavings more poignant every time.
And at the core it's not *our* house—
but hers, but mine, distinct to each.
For me, the thousand screws and nails,
the mitered join of cabinet and shelf,
the stage-set air of made-up rooms;
for her, the records, kitchen, looms—who knows?

Divorce has passed her back and forth between
opposing houses in the South. She'd learned
too early all the agnostic's tactful lies—
a Catholic deb in winter, alike awake
through roadhouse Saturday and Sunday Mass,
a gypsy tomboy on the cypress branch
of Baptist summer's grits & catfish camps.
So, two-homes homeless, and her nesting self
shunted to hobo spurs between the two,
she'd had no room to hoard her secrets in.

Myself, like others of my age and class,
I'd come to value family houses just
as I came to prize the faiths done in
by years of houses that were only lodgings.
I'd always longed for libraries

and dining rooms to take for granted—
a migrant bird with never time to roost,
forever moving elsewhere in the earnest farce
of loaded Plymouths in pre-dawn departures,
a stoicism bruised to life with acne.

Weary of cities where on rented ceilings
a flash of neon imitates the nerves,
once married we resembled separate sleepers
waking in each other's inmost dream,
resolved to find it in reality—
a quirky house to play house in.
For me, a place that could be made
ancestral; for her, an empty room
to fill with her odd loot—her jars
of Toenail shells, her cats, her Turner sky.

Our pack-rat caravansary became
a proof that continuity's what hinge
and saw and hammer (plus our hopes) assert.
Together, we restored the house, our sweat
and fantasy bequeathed us ownership—
the right to put off chores and loaf,
letting whatever fictive rest remains
affirm the final fact of houselessness:
        A home is where you have the chance
        of dying where you chose to live.

—*1986–1987*

Vignette

Down some mud alley
    in back of a Kansas town
on a night made memorable by rain,
    garbled curses red threats
      doomed inventions
made the night as extraordinary
    as news in a place where
      nothing happens
only a bitter boy choking on mud
    and the bittersweet dream
      the gunshot soured
and the yapping yellow dog

—1988

SWEET CHARITY

Walking down 3rd Avenue
in the 50s on a June morning,
a morning so good no one is
talking to themselves,
my shirt collar is as fresh as lettuce,
I have a good session
of words behind me;
there are twenty dollars in my wallet
to buy whatever midday taste I favor,
and my hangover is a not unpleasant large ache.
I am due to meet a friend
in Clarke's in twenty minutes.
I will be early
and will order a small martini,
then on to Annette's
where the *fines herbes* omelettes
are validated like passports
to Provence.
The thought
completes and crystallizes
my mood:
I am beyond happiness.
I wish for everything for everybody.

—1988

SAMOAN HEAD

Once, very sick,
late one night,
I saw the icon of a man
trying to breathe like me, his mouth
puckered for the sweet air—
to take it into his body
there in the South Pacific
five hundred years ago—
"A-h-h-h!" I breathed for him.

The last poem
written in the night
March 27, 1988